MW01206006

MY FIRST BOOK OF ELECTRICITY

By: Tom Fixit

THIS BOOK BELONGS TO:

Welcome to the world of electricity! This book is perfect for you and your parents to explore together. Get ready for fun, learning, and amazing discoveries!

THIS IS ELECTRICITY

Electricity is like tiny lightning bolts that travel through wires. Have you ever seen lightning in the sky?

FUN FACT!

Did You Know? Electricity travels at the speed of light!

MEET SPARK!

Meet Spark the Electrician. Spark loves to learn about electricity and how it powers our world!

SAFETY FIRST

Before we start learning about electricity, let's talk about safety. It's very important to stay safe when working with electricity.

SAFETY GEAR

- Helmet

Gloves-

-Eye protection

SAFETY RULES

- Always ask a grown-up for help.
- Keep water away from electrical devices.
- Never touch plugged-in wires.

TOOLS OF THE TRADE

FLAT HEAD

PHILLIPS

TOOL 1: A SCREWDRIVER!

This is a screwdriver. Electricians use it to tighten and loosen screws.

TOOLS OF THE TRADE

NEEDLE NOSE

SNAP RING

TOOL 2: PLIERS

These are pliers. They help electricians hold and bend wires.

TOOLS OF THE TRADE

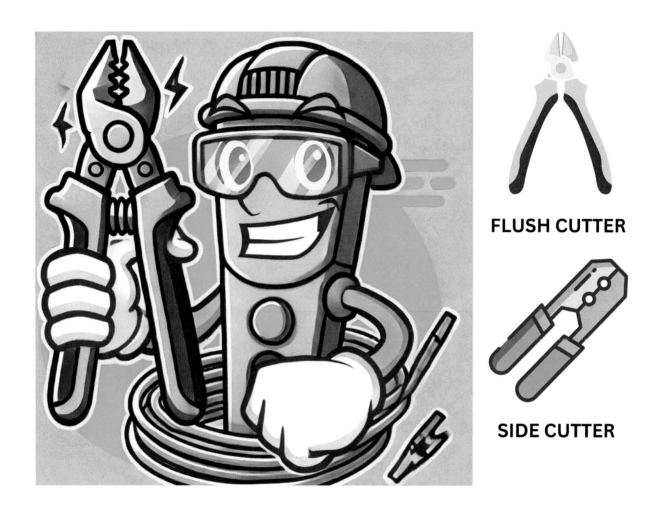

FLUSH CUTTER

SIDE CUTTER

TOOL 3: WIRE CUTTERS

Wire cutters are used to cut wires to the right length.

WHAT IS A CIRCUIT?

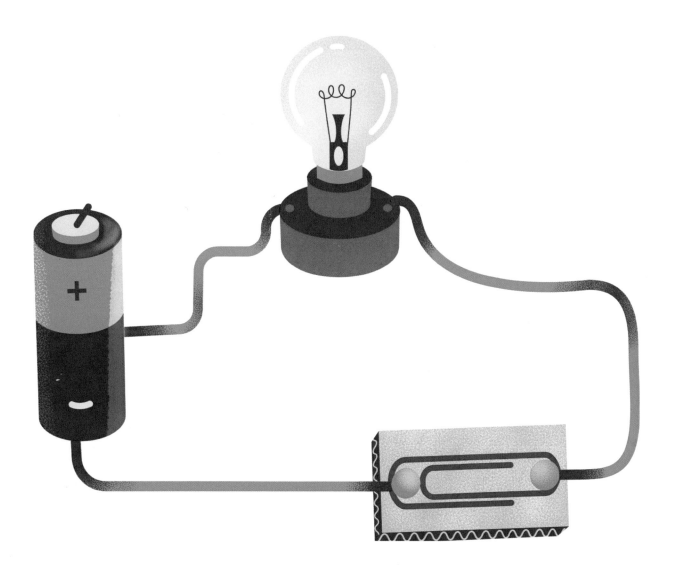

Electricity flows in a circle called a circuit. This makes the light bulb shine!

BUILDING A SIMPLE CIRCUIT

STEP 1: GATHER YOUR MATERIALS

Make sure you have a battery, wire, and a light bulb.

BUILDING A SIMPLE CIRCUIT
STEP 2: CONNECT THE WIRE TO THE BATTERY

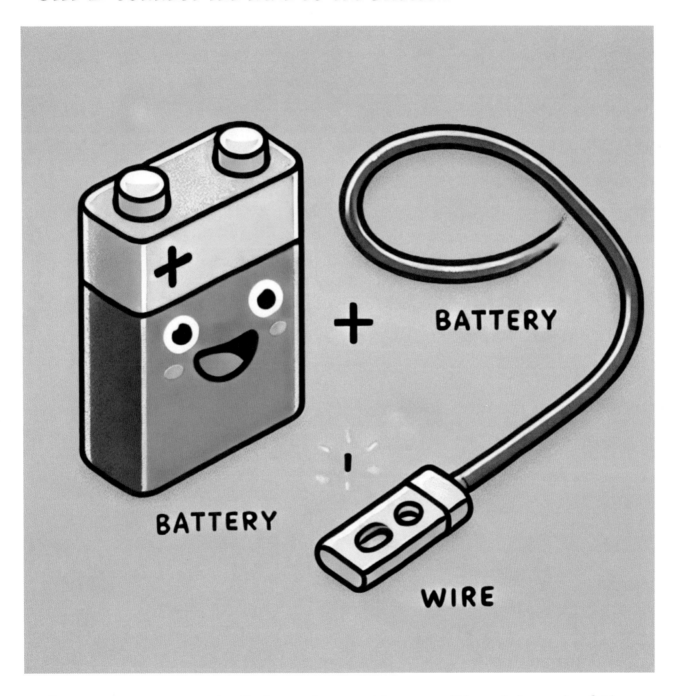

Connect one end of the wire to the positive (+) end of the battery.

BUILDING A SIMPLE CIRCUIT

STEP 3: CONNECT THE OTHER END OF THE BATTERY TO THE LIGHT BULB

Connect the other end of the wire to the metal base of the light bulb.

BUILDING A SIMPLE CIRCUIT

STEP 4: CONNECT ANOTHER WIRE TO THE LIGHT BULB

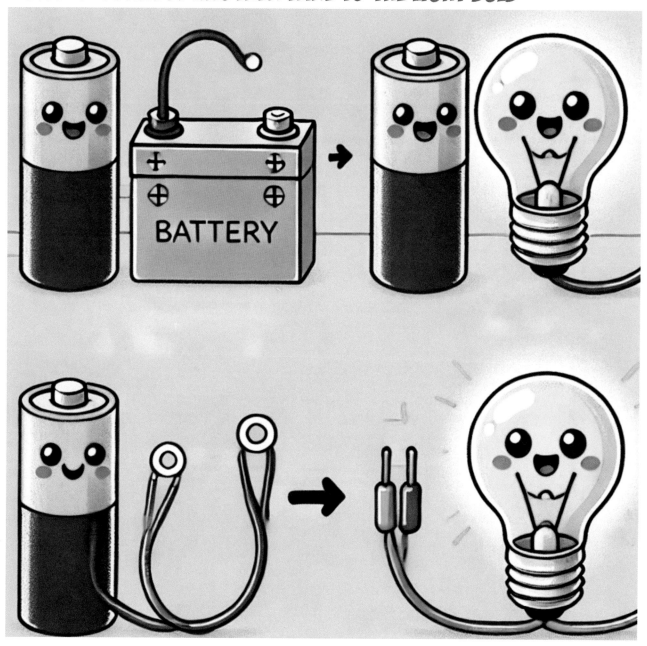

Take another wire and connect it to the other side of the metal base of the light bulb.

BUILDING A SIMPLE CIRCUIT
STEP 5: CONNECT THE SECOND WIRE TO THE BATTERY

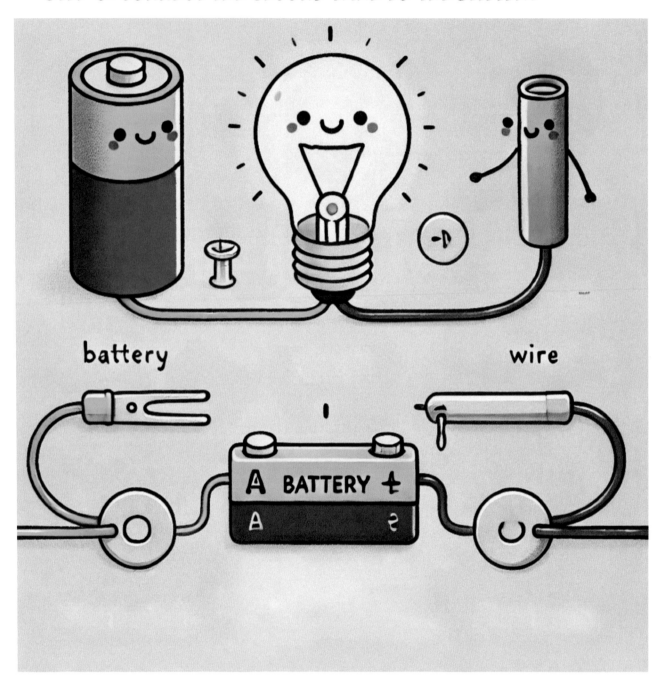

Finally, connect the other end of the second wire to the negative (-) end of the battery.

BUILDING A SIMPLE CIRCUIT

STEP 6: LIGHT UP!

Look, the light bulb is shining! You've made a simple circuit. Great job!

DIFFERENT SOURCES OF ELECTRICITY

Electricity can come from the sun, wind, and water!
Let's spot these sources in our world.

SOLAR POWER

Solar panels turn sunlight into electricity. How many solar panels can you find on your walk?

WIND POWER

Wind turbines use the wind to make electricity. Have you seen these big fans in fields or on TV?

HYDRO POWER

Dams use moving water to create electricity. Have you ever visited a dam?

ELECTRICITY IN OUR HOMES

We use electricity every day to power our homes and appliances. Which appliances do you use every day?

FUN FACT: STATIC ELECTRICITY

Did you know? Rubbing a balloon on your hair can create static electricity! Try it and see what happens.

FUN EXPERIMENT: CREATE A STATIC CHARGE

Try this fun experiment with a balloon and your hair!
Can you make your hair stand up?

MEET NIKOLA TESLA

This is Nikola Tesla. He was very smart and helped make electricity better for everyone.

MEET THOMAS EDISON

And this is Thomas Edison. He made the first light bulb that could shine for a long time!

What have you learned? Let's test your knowledge with a fun quiz! Can you answer these questions?

1. What Makes Light Bulbs Shine?
- Is it (A) Magic Dust or (B) Electricity?

2. Who Invented the First Light Bulb?
- Is it (A) Thomas Edison or (B) Nikola Tesla?

3. What Tool Do Electricians Use to Cut Wires?
- Is it (A) A Spoon or (B) Wire Cutters?

4. What Do You Call a Circle That Electricity Flows Through?
- Is it (A) A Circuit or (B) A Line?

5. What Does a Wind Turbine Use to Make Electricity?
- Is it (A) Water or (B) Wind?

6. Who Helped Improve Electricity for Everyone?
- Is it (A) Nikola Tesla or (B) Albert Einstein?

7. What Should You Always Ask for When Working with Electricity?
- Should you ask for (A) A Snack or (B) Help from a Grown-up?

8. What Can Create Static Electricity When Rubbed on Your Hair?
- Is it (A) A Balloon or (B) A Book?

SEE YOU NEXT TIME!

Thank you for exploring the world of electricity with Spark the Electrician! Keep learning and discovering new things every day!

Made in the USA
Las Vegas, NV
26 September 2024

95790523R00019